Leningrad

Leningrad

Aurora Art Publishers · Leningrad

Text by LEV USPENSKY

Compiled and designed by IRINA LUZHINA
and IGOR GORDEICHUK

© Aurora Art Publishers, Leningrad, 1987
Printed and bound in the USSR

Л $\frac{4902010000-473}{023(01)-87}$ 1-87

Some cities live quietly and peacefully for many centuries. Year after year they remain far removed from the tumultuous flow of historical events. Generations come and go, the years pass by, but nothing important, nothing truly earth-shaking ever happens. These cities intrude on no one, and no one intrudes on them. It is as if they hardly existed at all.

But there are cities of quite another kind. From the very first they seethe and boil without stopping. Their travails are heard around the world. They change with every passing year, and the changes remain indelibly etched on the fate of mankind. Rome was once such a city, Paris is now such a city, and Moscow, the capital and very heart of our country, is such a city. And, history tells us, Leningrad is one of these cities.

This city, "gem of the Northern world", has stood on the banks of the Neva for almost 300 years. This is not a very long time; there still are people living who are one-third as old as Leningrad. But what an infinity separates the Petersburg of the early eighteenth century — a frontier fort on a small island in a forest-lined, untamed river — from the stone, steel, and concrete giant of our times!

St. John Bridge
3

↑*View of the Peter and Paul Fortress*
1

Railings of Stroitelei (Builders') Bridge. Detail
2

1—7, 125. The cornerstone of the Peter and Paul Fortress was laid on May 16 (27, New Style), 1703, and it is from this day that the city dates its existence. From 1706 on, the original earthworks were gradually replaced by new structures in stone. The most striking building inside the fortress is the Cathedral of Sts Peter and Paul built to the design of Domenico Trezzini between 1712 and 1733. Its bell-tower was completed in 1723 and became one of the tallest points in the city's skyline. After the original timber frame of the spire was replaced by metal in 1857—58, the height of the spire reached 122.5 metres. In 1718, the fortress was turned into a political prison. Many revolutionaries and progressive figures of tsarist Russia were incarcerated in the Trubetskoi Bastion.

The Neva Gates of the Peter and Paul Fortress

5

6
The Peter and Paul
Fortress. In the distance,
entrance to the Trubetskoi
Bastion

7
Autumn. Cathedral
of Sts Peter and Paul

After the October Revolution the fortress was transformed into a museum (a section of the Museum of the History of Leningrad) dedicated to the heroism of Russian revolutionaries.

◁ Palace Embankment and the
Winter Palace from the Neva
8

Panoramic view
9

View of the Engineers' Castle
and the Field of Mars
▷ 10

View of Zagorodny Prospekt
11

Sculptural group topping
the House of Books
12

View of the Leningrad harbour
13

The city has had long years of unequal struggle, bright hopes and bitter disappointments. Its people have shed an ocean of tears. But now, the red star of the great revolution is proudly displayed on the broad chest of this northern colossus. Once the tsars' nameless slaves, exhausted by unbearable toil, died here without a murmur.

14. The Smolny building, a splendid example of early 19th-century Classicism, was built in 1806—8 by Giacomo Quarenghi to house a boarding-school for young ladies of noble birth. The name, Smolny, goes back to the early 18th century when a tar-yard (*smolianoi dvor*) was located here which stored tar for the city's shipyards. On October 24 (November 6, New Style), 1917, Smolny became the headquarters of the socialist revolution. From here Lenin supervised and direct-ed the October uprising from start to finish, including the assault and capture of the bourgeois Provisional Government's last stronghold — the Winter Palace.

When the *Aurora* fired its historic shot, the Second All-Russia Congress of Soviets was in session in the Assembly Hall of Smolny. The sittings were continued in the evening of October 26, and the Congress adopted the first decrees, proposed by Lenin, of the new régime — the Decree on Peace and the Decree on the Land. The Congress also approved the formation of the first ever workers' and peasants' government, the Council of People's Commis-

Museum of the October Revolution. Balcony 15

Propylaea at the entrance to Smolny 14

The entrance to the tree-lined avenue leading from Proletarian Dictatorship Square to Smolny is flanked with propylaea put up in 1924 to the design of Shchuko and Helfreich. They bear the inscriptions "The First Soviet of the Proletarian Dictatorship" and "Workers of All Countries, Unite!"

15, 16. The Museum of the October Revolution is housed in the former Kshesinskaya mansion (built in 1906 by A. Hogen), which from March to July 1917 served as the headquarters of the Central and Petrograd Committees of the Bolshevik Party. This is the house Lenin first came to on his return to Russia from abroad on April 3 (16, New Style), 1917, and it is from the balcony of this mansion that he repeatedly addressed the workers, soldiers, and sailors of Petrograd.

sars, with Lenin at its head.

Now the building houses the Regional and City Committees of the CPSU.

Smolny remained the seat of the Soviet Government till March 10, 1918.

Situated on the second floor of the building is the Lenin Memorial Museum.

In 1927, a statue of Lenin was set up in front of the portico (sculptor Vasily Kozlov, architect Vladimir Shchuko).

Now their grandchildren and great-grandchildren freely perform unparalleled feats of labour. Once the dry drum-rolls of Paul I's regiments resounded across the city's squares and the whistles of Arakcheyev's rods pierced the city's air. Now the living word is heard; now clear and correct thinking prevails; now the new life of which men

17. The Leningrad Branch of the Central Lenin Museum is housed in the former Marble Palace. Designed by Antonio Rinaldi and erected between 1768 and 1785, this palace is an early example of the Classical style in Russian architecture.

In 1937, the palace was given over to the Central Lenin Museum. In the inner garden of the palace is an armoured car with the words *The Enemy of Capital* inscribed on its turret. It is from this improvised stand that Lenin addressed a huge crowd of workers, soldiers, and sailors outside the Finland Station on April 3 (16, New Style), 1917.

The museum has a rich collection of articles and documents relating to the life and revolutionary activities of Lenin.

have dreamed for centuries is flourishing. Everyone who thinks back through the years will remember days of inspiration and elevation in his life. Such days are priceless, they make life worth living. Leningrad, too, has had such moments. The first was October 1917.

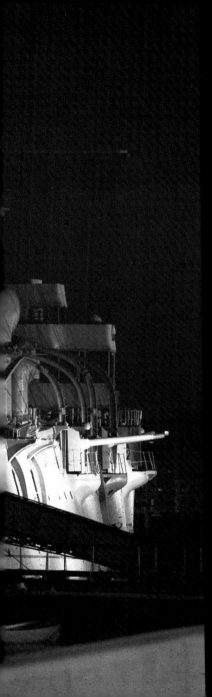

The cruiser Aurora
18

18. The cruiser *Aurora*, designed by Tokarevsky, entered service with the Russian Navy in 1903.
In the February revolution of 1917 the *Aurora* hoisted a red flag to express its support for the people's struggle.
On October 25 (November 7, New Style), 1917, the cruiser, acting in accordance with Lenin's plan for armed uprising, approached Nikolayevsky Bridge (now Lt. Schmidt Bridge) on the Neva and aimed its guns at the Winter Palace. At 9:45 p.m. it fired the historic shot that signalled the storming of the Winter Palace. On November 17, 1948, the *Aurora*, a revered relic of the October Revolution, was moored permanently in the Bolshaya Nevka opposite the Nakhimov Naval School.
In 1956, the cruiser was converted into a branch of the Central Naval Museum.

The fate of the October Revolution was decided on the streets of Petrograd (as the city was known from 1914 to 1924). Here, the first regiments of the Red Army were formed to defend the new freedom and to vanquish the old world once and for all.

> They blew as always,
>   October's
>   winds,
>   as cold as capitalism
>   their icy blast.
>
> Over Troitsky Bridge
>   sped
>   cars and trams,
>   snaking along
>   the rails
>   of the past.

These are the words used by the poet Vladimir Mayakovsky to describe the day preceding the onset of the new era ushered in by the storming of the Winter Palace and the victory of the October Revolution. To my mind, the most amazing aspect of it all is that for the inhabitants of Petrograd this was a day like any other, "a day as always". There was the usual grey October sky lowering over the city, a sky by now rainless but not yet snow-filled. "Over Troitsky Bridge" (as Kirovsky Bridge was then called) sped automobiles and trams, and thousands upon thousands of people were crossing it as well... And many were completely unaware of the turning-point their lives, the life of the country, the life of the world were approaching. Could they have foreseen the future they would have tried to capture and store in their memories every single moment, every minute particular of that day. Most of them, however, knew nothing as yet... Or almost nothing. There was a feeling in the air that another collision between revolution and counter-revolution was about to erupt, just "another", not the first, and if not the first, then most likely not the decisive one either. Only Lenin and the Military Revolutionary Committee knew, and the Red Guards, the soldiers and workers already fighting in various parts of the city or massing in the vicinity of the Winter Palace knew or guessed what was about to happen. As evening approached, the autumn gloom solidified. Sinister and ominous stretched the huge expanse of Palace Square; the Winter Palace loomed in the night like a new Bastille... With every hour the new day was drawing closer, the first day of a great historic epoch.

It was these historic days that subsequently earned Petrograd its greatest reward: the name "Leningrad", a proud memorial to the greatest Russian — Vladimir Ilyich Lenin.

Our city has long been known as Russia's "window to the West". From 1917, it has been called the cradle of the proletarian revolution. The city's character reflects both: its role as window to the West and its role as first city of the revolution.

The perfection of the city's architecture embodies the best traditions and aspirations of its builders. History and architecture, granite and poetry have become one. Here you will see not only monuments standing on city squares and in the city's buildings; you will see city squares that are themselves monuments, buildings that are monuments, and avenues that are monuments. For it was precisely on them and in them that the history of our great country was played out.

Take, for example, the square in front of Finland Station. No rifle shots or gunfire were heard here. But on April 3, 1917, Lenin, having just returned from exile abroad, uttered his first thunderous words to the workers of Petrograd, to the workers, peasants, and soldiers of the entire country.

"Down with the imperialist war!"

"Long live the socialist revolution!"

Many citizens — most of the intelligentsia, officials, and scientists — knew the name of Lenin, but for them it hardly meant anything. Only the workers and soldiers knew that this name was all-important; it meant their very existence.

A great welcoming crowd gathered in the square in front of the Finland Station. Lenin climbed onto the turret of an armoured car and, as he faced the city and, as it were, Russia itself, he proclaimed these slogans, which thundered across the country all the way south to the Black Sea and all the way east to Vladivostok. His words found a response in the heart of every worker and every soldier. They made their way into the countryside, to the millions of uneducated and downtrodden Russian peasants. His

Monument to Lenin in front
of the Finland Railway Station.
Detail
19

19. The monument to Lenin in front of the Finland Station (designed by Sergei Yevseyev; architects Vladimir Shchuko and Vladimir Helfreich), one of the earliest works of Soviet monumental art, was unveiled on November 7, 1926.

In 1945—46, it was moved closer to the Neva and became the compositional centre of a newly created square.

words gave them hope for rapid changes, but, most of all, a willingness to go and conquer the future, sparing neither their blood nor their lives.

Now on this square stands a monument to Lenin. Designed by the sculptor Sergei Yevseyev and the architect Vladimir Shchuko, it is probably the only statue in the world whose base is an armoured-car turret, or more accurately, a bronze replica of a turret. In the statue, the artists have managed to capture the historic moment: Lenin standing with his back to the station and to the long years of forced exile he was leaving behind forever. His face and raised arm are turned to his native land, to Russia, to its people and future. This is a remarkable monument to the great revolutionary, the man who literally fashioned a new world, the world of socialism.

Arch of the General Staff building

Consider yet another of the city's squares — the Field of Mars. It was once a gigantic military parade ground. The wind off the Neva blew in and raised clouds of sand and red dust. Now it is a beautiful garden, flooded in spring by a sea of white and purple lilacs. It is the resting place of the heroes of the February and October

revolutions. In its centre burns an eternal flame. The Field of Mars is thus a monument to the Revolution as well as one of the most beautiful parts of the city. It is lovely by day and enchanting by night, when it is bathed in the light of the garden's many street-lamps; and sadly pensive during the white nights. The Swan Canal flows

21. The Field of Mars used to be called at different times the Amusement Field (because of "amusement lights" or fire-crackers set off here during court festivities) and the Tsarina's Meadow (because Catherine I's palace was situated close by). Later it came to be called the Field of Mars because of the military parades and reviews held here from the late 18th century onwards.

In 1917, the fallen heroes of the February and October revolutions were interred here; in 1918, Volodarsky and Uritsky, assassinated by socialist-revolutionary terrorists, as well as Petrograd workers who died in Yaroslavl defending the socialist cause against counter-revolutionary armed insurrection.

In 1917—19, a memorial dedicated to the heroes of the Revolution was built here to the design of Lev Rudnev.

quietly just to its east, and, beyond it, the marble statues of the Summer Gardens repose in ageless slumber.

The railings on the Neva side of the Summer Gardens are among the world's finest.

Many of the city's older residents may remember an old, purely Petersburg story.

At the end of the 1850s, an old schooner entered the mouth of the Neva and dropped anchor below the nearest bridge. A small boat then cast off from the schooner and moved upstream. As it passed the place

In 1920—23, the Field of Mars was replanned by I. Fomin, with paths, lawns, and gardens.
In 1957, on the eve of the 40th anniversary of the October Revolution, an eternal flame was lit here. The dark-grey granite platform and burner were designed by E. Maiofis.

22—30, 104. The Summer Gardens and the Summer Palace of Peter the Great are magnificent examples of early 18th-century Russian architecture and landscape gardening.
The Gardens were laid out in 1704 in the formal style by Jan Roosen, Schroeder, Surmin, Lukyanov, Yakovlev, Niccolo Michetti, Jean-Baptiste Le Blond, Matveyev, Zemtsov, and others. The geometric lay-out of the Gardens' avenues and walks and their unique collection of marble statuary by early 18th-century Italian masters have been preserved intact.

where the Swan Canal flows out of the Neva, it moored. Its owner walked out onto the quay near the gate of the Summer Gardens. He suddenly stopped and stood still, never taking his eyes off the Gardens' famous wrought-iron railings designed by Yury Velten. For no less than an hour he remained rooted to the spot, with a strange

23
The Summer Palace of Peter the Great

24
View from the window of the Summer Palace

The railings of magnificent ironwork on the Neva side of the Gardens were designed by Yury Velten and Piotr Yegorov and erected in 1784. The modest two-storey Summer Palace of Peter the Great, in the northeast corner of the Summer Gardens, was built by Domenico Trezzini in 1710—12. It was transformed into a museum in 1934. On display in its rooms are works of fine and applied art, furniture and utility items characteristic of palace interiors in the first quarter of the 18th century.

look fixed on his face, a look that might well have appeared on Salieri's face as he listened to Mozart, a look of admiration and envy.

He then walked along the fence, turned round, and fell into thought. There were only a few people strolling in the Gardens. One, more curious than the others, came

The Summer Gardens. Night

up to him and asked politely, "May I be of service, my dear sir?"

"No!" the man retorted. "It is simply too beautiful. A thousand times more than all the drawings and prints of it I've seen. For many years I've wanted to find out why its charm is so indescribable. Now I can see it myself. Look at the gilded handles on the vases atop its granite pillars. On one vase they turn down, on the two flanking ones they turn up. I'm no Rothschild, but I bought a schooner and sailed here to find out just exactly why this is such a work of genius. Now I know, and there's no reason to stay any longer. Farewell, sir!"

"Adieu, sir!" replied the inquisitive passer-by. It is believed that the latter was the Russian writer Goncharov, but no one really knows for sure.

I have told this story so that the reader can understand what kind of city he will be seeing in this book. The great Dostoyevsky with good reason called it the most contrived, the most fantastical city in the world; and Pushkin, Russia's greatest poet, sang a paean to it in *The Bronze Horseman,* a poetic encyclopaedia of its splendour.

Gates of the Summer Gardens

30

Compared to other large cities, Leningrad is a mere youngster, only ninety-odd years older than Washington. Peter the Great founded the city on May 16, 1703. Ten years later, St. Petersburg looked just about as Paris must have looked in the first few centuries A.D., consisting only of an island fortress and a handful of low buildings

first third of the 18th century, was built between 1718 and 1734 by Nikolaus Herbel, Gaetano Chiaveri, Georg Johann Mattarnovi, and Mikhail Zemtsov. In 1747, it was damaged by fire and restored by Savva

the first national museum. Its ethnographic collections are devoted to the history, economy, architecture, and artistic handicrafts of the peoples of Asia, Africa, America, and Australia.

Next door to the *Kunstkammer* stands the building of the Academy of Sciences designed by Giacomo Quarenghi and set up in 1783—89. It is one of the most remarkable examples of Russian Classicism.

31. The building of the Museum of Anthropology and Ethnography of the USSR Academy of Sciences (the former *Kunstkammer*), an early example of Russian architecture of the Chevakinsky, who simplified the original design. The peaked superstructure of the tower was recreated in the course of restoration work in 1947—48. The *Kunstkammer* was

32. The Menshikov Palace was built for Alexander Menshikov, companion and adviser of Peter the Great, as part of a spacious estate, in the 1720s by Domenico Fontana and Gottfried Schädel. One of the first stone structures of St. Petersburg, it far exceeded in size and splendour all other buildings in the new capital. In spite of numerous alterations effected in the course of the 18th century, the palace has on the whole retained its original aspect. The interior decoration of some of the halls on the first floor has also been preserved inviolate. Now the palace houses a branch of the Hermitage — the Department of Russian Applied Art.

stretching out along the banks of the river. Now Leningrad is not quite three centuries old. Nevertheless, it is one of the ten largest cities in the world.

33. A handsome palace-type stone building, the Kikin Mansion, dates from the early 18th century. Its first owner was Kikin, an associate of Peter the Great. After being damaged during the War of 1941—45, the Kikin Mansion was restored to its original appearance by the architect Irina Benois in the early 1950s.

34, 35. The Twelve Collegia building is a splendid example of civic architecture in the first third of the 18th century. It was built between 1722 and 1742 by Domenico Trezzini and Theodor Schwertfeger to house Russia's supreme government ministries —

the Senate and the collegia. According to the main architectural rule of the Petrine epoch, the terrace of twelve pavilion-like buildings, each with a high hipped roof, is united by a common façade. In 1835, the entire collegia complex was assigned to the university. This called for certain alterations, which were effected by Apollon Shchedrin. St. Petersburg University made a significant contribution to the development of Russian science and played a major role in the revolutionary movement of the late 19th and early 20th centuries. It was the *Alma Mater* of many illustrious figures in the country's sciences and arts — Mechnikov, Pavlov, Mendeleyev, Chernyshevsky, Blok, and others. In 1891, Lenin sat for his examinations here after completing an extramural course in law.

Palace Square with the Winter Palace and Alexander Column

36

36. Palace Square, one of the oldest squares in Leningrad, serves as a parade ground during the celebration of state and revolutionary holidays. The ensemble of the square was created in the course of two centuries by several generations of architects.

The Winter Palace, a typical Baroque structure, was designed by Bartolommeo Rastrelli and erected during the years 1754—62. It was constructed round a large inner courtyard with fine façades facing the Neva, the Admiralty and Palace Square. The façade overlooking the river is 230 metres in length. After the February revolution that overthrew the tsarist régime, the palace was for a short time the seat of the counter-revolutionary Provisional Government. On the night of October 25 (November 7, New Style), 1917, the Winter Palace was taken by storm by revolutionary workers, soldiers and sailors, and it was here that the Provisional Government was deposed.

Today the Winter Palace is one of the buildings that make up the Hermitage, whose collections enjoy world renown. The centrepiece of Palace Square, the 47.5-metre-tall Alexander Column, commemorates Russia's victory over Napoleon in the War of 1812—14. It was built in 1829—34 from a design of Auguste Montferrand. The pedestal of the column is adorned with bronze compositions in relief executed by P. Svintsov, I. Leppe and S. Balin after drawings by Montferrand and Giovanni Battista Scotti. The column is crowned by the figure of an angel holding a cross in one hand, the work of Boris Orlovsky. The column was hewed out of a dark-red granite monolith under the supervision of the talented stonemason Yakovlev. It is kept secure on the pedestal entirely by its own weight.

Porch of the New Hermitage
37

37, 38. The New Hermitage, the work of Leo von Klenze, was built between 1842 and 1851. Its main façade is notable for a porch supported by granite atlantes carved after the models of Alexander Terebenev. The Winter Canal connects the Neva with the Moika. It got its name from an earlier Winter Palace, built here in the 18th century for Peter the Great and later, in 1783—87, replaced by the Hermitage Theatre designed by Giacomo Quarenghi. A roofed passage connects the Hermitage Theatre with the Old Hermitage.

Cathedral of the former Smolny Convent (Branch of the History of Leningrad Museum)

39, 40. The cathedral of the former Smolny Convent, designed by Bartolommeo Rastrelli, is an outstanding example of Russian architecture in the mid-18th century. Its construction was begun in 1748 and completed in the rough in 1764. The final stage of the construction and the interior decoration were effected by Vasily Stasov in 1832—35. Now the cathedral houses a branch of the Museum of the History of Leningrad.

Youthful cities such as Leningrad seldom acquire "character". This usually takes hundreds, even thousands of years. The same is also true of statues and buildings: the Venus of Milo and the Acropolis would not be quite so interesting if they did not bear the marks of a long, long life. Most cities, too, need time before countless

generations can mould their character. The most marvellous thing about Leningrad is that the rule does not hold true. The city was founded fairly recently, and, it may have seemed, in defiance of all reason: that is, on the swampy banks of a wild river, amidst dense forests, and between a sea gulf and an enormous lake, both of which

41, 42. The Stroganov Palace was designed by Bartolommeo Rastrelli. The work was carried out in 1752—54. It is one of the finest buildings on Nevsky Prospekt, with frontage both to the Moika Embankment and Nevsky Prospekt. The little garden in the inner courtyard is decorated with sculpture.
The Stroganov Palace was rebuilt in the 1790s by Andrei Voronikhin.

are ice-bound almost half the year. But the city's vital force could not be held in check.

> A century — and the city young,
> Gem of the Northern world, amazing,
> From gloomy wood and swamp upsprung,
> Had risen, in pride and splendour blazing.

(Alexander Pushkin,
The Bronze Horseman.
Translated by Oliver Elton)

The Sheremetev Palace
43

*Inner courtyard
of the Stroganov Palace*
42

43. The Sheremetev Palace was built in 1750—55 by Savva Chevakinsky and Fiodor Argunov. Compositionally this is a typical manor house with a courtyard and a garden at the back. The manor grounds are fenced off from the Fontanka Embankment by a cast-iron railing (architect Geronimo Corsini, late 1830s). The decoration of the façades is a blend of traditional Petrine elements with moulded window surrounds, leonine masks and elaborate capitals characteristic of the Baroque style.

Now the building houses the Institute of the Arctic and Antarctic.

45
*Railings of
the Rumiantsev Garden. Detail*

44. The building of the Academy of Art, one of the first examples of Russian Classicism, was put up between 1764 and 1788 by Alexander Kokorinov and Vallin de la Mothe. Among the graduates of the Academy are many painters, sculptors, engravers, and architects, who have earned fame for Russian and Soviet art.

46. The origination of the New Holland ensemble is connected with the development of St. Petersburg as a shipbuilding centre on the Baltic Sea. The little island, called New Holland in Peter the Great's time, came into being following the digging of the Admiralty and Kriukov Canals. In 1765, Savva Chevakinsky built several brick warehouses here for storing timber. The façades of these buildings and the arch over the canal that flows into a pool inside the island were designed by Jean-Baptiste Vallin de la Mothe. The granite Tuscan columns are strictly classical in their proportions.

It is quite understandable that a northern Gibraltar, a major naval base, has grown up here. It is only natural for the noisy docks of a busy trading port to have sprung up here. Nor would it have been surprising if Petersburg, having reached its centenary, had turned into a "central office", a heap of odd structures and administrative

47. The Tauride Palace, a remarkable example of Russian Classicism, was built between 1783 and 1789 by Ivan Starov. It was here that on April 4 (17, New Style), 1917, Lenin read out his famous April Theses at a meeting of Bolshevik delegates to the All-Russia Conference of Soviets of Workers' and Soldiers' Deputies.

buildings needed to rule a colossal empire. But the beginnings of the new capital coincided with a decisive turning-point in the history of the country. The old Muscovite Russia disappeared, and a new Imperial Russia took its place. A little-known country, which only yesterday had seemed as far away as Asia, took its place among

48, 112. The building of the Institute of Finance and Economics (the former State Bank), an outstanding example of Russian architecture of the last third of the 18th century, was designed by Giacomo Quarenghi and built between 1783 and 1790. Features typical of Russian suburban estates are very much in evidence here.

49. The Chesme Church, built in 1777—80 by Yury Velten, is one of the few pseudo-Gothic structures in Leningrad architecture. Its name comes from the great naval victory of 1770 over the Turks in the Aegean at Chesme. The décor of the façades is based on an arbitra-

the European powers, moving proudly to the very centre of European life.

It is for this very reason, evidently, that the new city became something quite unique, something of a Wunderstadt. In two centuries it had traversed the same stormy and treacherous road it had taken the other world capitals a thousand years to cover.

49
The Chesme Church (Museum "Victory of Chesme")

ry treatment of Gothic motifs.

The church was restored in 1965—68. Now it houses the Leningrad Branch of the Central Naval Museum.

50. The Engineers' (Mikhailovsky) Castle, a remarkable monument of late 18th-century Russian architecture, was designed by Vasily Bazhenov and built between 1797 and 1800 by Vincenzo Brenna as a sort of fortified residence: it was surrounded by two rivers, the Fontanka and Moika, and moats.

In 1823, the castle was given over to the School of Military Engineers (hence the name Engineers' Castle). Among its graduates over the years were Dostoyevsky, Kondratenko, a hero of the Russo-Japanese War, and the fortifications engineer Karbyshev, Hero of the Soviet Union.

51, 52. The Cathedral of Our Lady of Kazan, an architectural monument of Russian Classicism, was designed and built between 1801 and 1811 by Andrei Voronikhin. In designing the building the architect had to solve a number of difficult problems. He found, for instance, a bold solution of harmonizing the new edifice with the already existing buildings while making it a dominant feature of the whole area. A semicircular court is formed in front of the cathedral by its majestic yet graceful colonnades

linking the build-
ing with Nevsky
Prospekt. This impres-
sive arc of Corinthian
columns, 96 in num-
ber, is the most re-
markable feature
of Voronikhin design.
The ornamentation of
the cathedral façades
is the work of the
finest sculptors of the
time — Stepan Pime-
nov, Ivan Martos,
Ivan Prokofyev, Vasi-
ly Demuth-Malinovsky,
and Fiodor Gordeyev.
The cathedral stands
about 70 metres high.
Its facing, pilasters,
columns, and elements
of its sculptural décor
are all done in pale-
yellow Pudost stone.
After the War of 1812—
14 the cathedral became
a pantheon of Russian
military glory: in 1813,
the remains of Field
Marshal Kutuzov were
transferred to the
cathedral.
Now the cathedral
serves as premises to
the USSR Academy of
Sciences' Museum of
the History of Reli-
gion and Atheism.

The Neva with the Admiralty in the distance
53

53—55. The magnificent building of the Admiralty, one of the supreme achievements of Russian Classicism, is the architectural and compositional pivot of the city. Its present-day look took about a hundred years to achieve. Construction of the first Admiralty (a fortified shipyard) was begun in 1704. The second was designed by Ivan Korobov and erected between 1727 and 1738. The now existing Admiralty building was put up in 1806—23 to the design of Adrian Zakharov.

The main façade runs parallel to Admiralty Prospekt; in the centre of the building is a graceful tower topped by a gilt spire (72.5 metres high overall) with a weather-vane in the shape of a caravel on its tip. Flanking the central arch are two sculptural groups of sea nymphs supporting the Earth's sphere. In the latter half of the 19th century, the territory of the former shipyard was taken up by residential buildings which shut the Admiralty off from the Neva embankment. Access to the Neva is through the archways of two symmetrically situated pavilions. An integral part of

Central part of the Admiralty
54

The Admiralty.
Sculptural group at the entrance
55

the Admiralty's architecture is its sculptured décor, which accentuates the building's *raison d'être* navigation and shipbuilding. Eminent Russian sculptors, Fiodor Shchedrin, Ivan Terebenev, Stepan Pimenov, Vasily Demuth-Malinovsky, and Artemy Anisimov, took part in its decoration.

The city came to maturity — an architectural and poetic gem. I must here allow myself the pleasure of saying that one square kilometre of this city is no less rich aesthetically than any similar area in any of the famous cities of the world and, furthermore, that its aesthetic potential is second to none.

56—58. One of the first large ensembles to appear on the banks of the Neva was the complex on the spit of Vasilyevsky Island. In the latter half of the 18th century, the main port of St. Petersburg was founded on the spit, where earlier there were country estates and saw-mills, and still earlier, in the first decade of the 18th century, fortifications.

The Stock Exchange building and two rostral columns, erected by Thomas de Thomon in 1805—10, became the centrepiece of the architectural ensemble of the spit. The bases of the rostral columns are grey granite, and the columns themselves are built of blocks of Pudost stone and decorated with ship's prows. The seated figures represent the four great Russian rivers — the Volga, Dnieper, Neva and Volkhov. They were designed by an anonymous artist and carved out of Pudost stone

This veritable museum of a city lies on the sixtieth parallel, the same latitude as southern Greenland. If you come to visit us in June, you will probably not manage to fall asleep the first night. You will be waiting for it to get dark, but, even though the sun will set, it will not get any darker. At midnight you can read a book by the by Samson Sukhanov. Installed on the columns are cup-like burners resting on tripods, and on festive days huge tongues of flame rise skyward from their tops. Housed here is the Central Naval Museum, one of the oldest museums in Russia, which came into being almost simultaneously with the birth of the city.

window without having to turn on the lights. But it is not really so strange after all; for at 3:45 a.m. the sun will once again appear on the horizon. The entire night, this enchanting white night, will last only five hours and twenty-six minutes. On such a night, the city seems to sink into a silvery-blue haze that comes from nowhere.

Lovers will be strolling along the banks of the river. On the stone seats along the quays, university students will be cramming for exams on the resistance of materials and theoretical mechanics. When the school year ends, the happy graduates will dance and sing all night long by the Neva.

58
↑ *The Spit of Vasilyevsky Island*

59
Stroitelei (Builders') Bridge across the Malaya Neva

*Church of St. Catherine
on Vasilyevsky Island*
60

*Descent on the Spit
of Vasilyevsky Island*
61

*Pediment of the Stock
Exchange. Detail*
62

63
A granite vase decorating
the Admiralty Embankment

64
A bronze lion decorating
the Admiralty Embankment

Details of railings
65, 66

Dvortsovy (Palace)
Bridge across the Neva
67

72. Malokoniushenny and Teatralny (Theatre) Bridges, designed by Yegor Adam and Georges Traitteur and built in 1829—31, constitute an interesting ensemble, the only one of its kind in the world. Teatralny Bridge spanning the Moika River is positioned dead along the axis of the Yekaterininsky (now Griboyedov) Canal, and leading up to it from both banks of the canal are two drives which make up Malokoniushenny Bridge. The whole ensemble was referred to in those days as the "triple arch" bridge.

73
Kriukov Canal. Bell-tower
of St. Nicholas's Cathedral

74
Lomonosov
Bridge across the Fontanka

The Moika
75

73. The Cathedral of St. Nicholas was built in 1753—62 by Savva Chevakinsky and represents a fine example of the Russian Baroque. Nearby, on the Kriukov Canal, stands the detached bell-tower, an elegant four-tiered structure, also by Chevakinsky.

74. Lomonosov (Chernyshov) Bridge was built in 1785—87 by A. Viazemsky. This three-span bridge was similar in design to the stone bridges that then spanned the Fontanka. Granite towers topped by domes were erected on the piers of the bridge, and placed inside them were special mechanisms for raising the central span to allow the passage of sailing vessels. In the mid-19th century, the bascule bridges over the Fontanka were reconstructed: the turrets were pulled down and the machinery for manipulating the bascule was removed. In that respect Lomonosov Bridge was least affected: in 1912, it was rebuilt into a cantilever bridge on metal beams, but its turrets remained intact. The granite obelisks with lamps and figured corbels were restored in 1950.

Or, if you wish, visit us in winter:

> I love thy ruthless winter, lowering
> With bitter frost and windless air;
> The sledges along Neva scouring;
> Girls' cheeks — no rose so bright and fair!
>
> (Alexander Pushkin, *The Bronze Horseman*.
> Translated by Oliver Elton)

building on Sadovaya Street
76

77
Sailing vessels by
the Neva embankment

The Neva sculpture
at the base of
a rostral column
78

A sphinx decorating
the University
Embankment
80

A sphinx decorating
the Sverdlov
Embankment
79

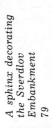

81. St. Isaac's Cathedral was built between 1818 and 1858 after the design of Auguste Montferrand. Many-columned porticos surround this monumental structure on all four sides. The monolithic granite columns are 17 metres high. The pediments of the porticos are decorated with reliefs representing religious subjects. The sculptural décor of the edifice consists of about four hundred pieces executed by Ivan Vitali, Nikolai Pimenov, Piotr Klodt, and Alexander Loganovsky.

The cathedral is surmounted by a tall drum crowned by a gilded dome with an octagonal lantern. The four smaller cupolas serve as bell-towers. The walls of the cathedral are faced with marble. Its overall height is 101.5 metres.

In 1931, the cathedral was converted into a museum. Numerous schemes, documents, models, and mock-ups speak of the work performed by the talented and ingenious architects, engineers, stonemasons, and founders who erected this edifice, and of the back-breaking toil by scores of thousands of serfs that the project entailed.

You will not see sledges gliding along the Neva; after all, we live in the age of the automobile! But the "windless air" and "bitter frost" and the rose-red cheeks are still here, along with countless architectural marvels, of which the railings of the Summer Gardens are not the best by far.

82. The equestrian statue of Peter the Great on Decembrists' Square, known as the Bronze Horseman (after Pushkin's poem of the same name) is one of the finest achievements of monumental sculpture. It was created in 1782 by Etienne-Maurice Falconet. The pedestal of the statue is a granite rock 8 metres high and weighing 1,600 tons.

84, 86. According to Carlo Rossi's design, approved in 1845, a wide boulevard (now Boulevard Profsoyuzov) was laid out, where there was once the Admiralty Canal linking the Admiralty with the New Holland arch. The marble columns on either side of the boulevard were erected between the present Main Exhibition Hall (the former Horse Guards Manège) and the Central Historical Archives (the former Synod) in 1845—46. The polished

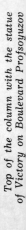

View of Leningrad with St. Isaac's Cathedral and the Admiralty
83

Top of the column with the statue of Victory on Boulevard Profsoyuzov

columns and pedestals were carved out of monoliths of Serdobol granite. The bronze statues crowning them were cast in the Berlin workshop of Christian Daniel Rauch after sketches by Rossi.

and the trophies decorating the Arch were modelled by Boris Orlovsky. The monument was inaugurated on October 16, 1838. It was the largest cast-iron structure in the world at that time.

85
University Embankment

Columns topped with statues
of Victory on Boulevard
Profsoyuzov
86

Moscow
Triumphal
Arch
87

Lamp in the garden
on Ostrovsky Square
88

The Russian Museum from
the Mikhailovsky Garden
89

89. The Mikhailovsky Palace (now the Russian Museum) was built in 1819—25 by Carlo Rossi in a classically clear-cut style typical of the urban estates of the nobility. After the area adjoining the palace was replanned, it became a compositional pivot of the architectural ensemble on Mikhailovskaya Square (now Arts Square). Stepan Pimenov and Vasily Demuth-Malinovsky were responsible for the many reliefs which decorate the building. In 1895, the palace was converted into the Russian Museum, which is now one of the country's largest depositories of paintings, sculptures, drawings, and works of applied arts by Russian and Soviet artists.

90. Carlo Rossi designed two squares — Alexandrinskaya (now Ostrovsky) Square and Chernyshov (now Lomonosov) Square — and a street behind the Alexandrinsky Theatre (now Pushkin Drama Theatre) linking these squares. Later, this street, which originally was called Teatralnaya, was renamed Rossi Street. The plan envisaged by Rossi for this area did not fully materialize.

Lomonosov Square 90

In the 1870s, a small garden was laid out in Chernyshov Square. In 1892, a bust of Lomonosov, the great Russian scientist whose name the square now bears, was installed in the centre of this garden. It was modelled by Zabello.

91. The statue of Pushkin on Arts Square, the work of Mikhail Anikushin, is one of the best monuments to the great Russian poet. It was unveiled in 1957. The granite pedestal was designed by Vasily Petrov.

92, 94. The balanced proportions and the classical beauty of Rossi Street (formerly Teatralnaya Street) make it a real masterpiece of urban architecture. The identical buildings lining the street on both sides make an artistic whole with the south façade of the Pushkin Drama Theatre.

93. The Rossi Pavilion was built by Carlo Rossi in 1825. It stands on the bank of the Moika in the Mikhailovsky Garden bordering on the Mikhailovsky Palace grounds. The granite terrace on the Moika bank is surrounded by cast-iron fence executed after a drawing by Rossi.

Rossi Street
92

The Rossi Pavilion
in the Mikhailovsky Garden
93

Rossi Street near the Pushkin
Drama Theatre
94

Palace Square. The General Staff building and the Alexander Column

95

95. The General Staff building, designed by Carlo Rossi, was erected between 1819 and 1829 to house the General Staff and two government ministries — finance and foreign affairs. The imposing edifice with its semi-circle of curvilinear blocks fronts a large square before the Winter Palace. In the centre of the almost six-hundred-metre-long façade is a triumphal arch, a monument to the Russia's victory over Napoleon in the War of 1812—14. The sides of the archway are ornamented with trophies. Crowning the arch is the winged figure of Victory driving a six-horse chariot. The authors of these sculptures were Stepan Pimenov and Vasily Demuth-Malinovsky.

And so, you are drawing closer to Leningrad. I have no idea how you may come, by land, sea, or air. As for me, I would rather come by sea or air. Each way has its own charm.

96 *The Pushkin Drama Theatre*

96. The Pushkin Drama Theatre (the former Alexandrinsky Theatre), one of the most outstanding architectural monuments of Russian Classicism, was designed

A major role in the decoration of the façade belongs to sculptures by Stepan Pimenov, Vasily Demuth-Malinovsky, and Alessandro Triscorni. The chariot of Apollo was made

Lamps decorating façade of the Maly Opera and Ballet Theatre

97

...ce Embankment

If you have chosen to come by air, it is best to come when it's dark. Of course, you have probably flown at dusk or at night into the large cities of the world. You know the shining array of city lights, those constellations and galaxies that twinkle up through the thick fog. Leningrad, too, is a

starry firmament come down to earth. Seen from the air, it spreads over its many islands like a gigantic hand, the deep and inky waters of the Neva rushing on between its island fingers. Further to the west, a solid area of black begins — this is the Gulf of Finland.

100. In the 1970s, a group of apartment houses was built on the Sverdlov Embankment of the Neva, opposite the former Smolny Convent. A. Vasilyev was the architect in charge of the project. A particularly striking impression is produced by six nine-storey houses standing in two parallel lines between the Sverdlov Embankment and Bolsheokhtinsky Prospekt.

101. The Port Arrival and Departure building was designed by a group of architects under the supervision of V. Sokhin and constructed in 1982 by A. Nelipa and A. Fedorovich.
The walls of the building are faced with relief-work panels, which look like sails filled out with wind. It is topped by a tower with a 74-metre spire.

ЛЕНИНГРАД

103. The Hotel Leningrad was designed by S. Speransky, N. Kamensky, and V. Struzman, with the participation of V. Volonsevich, S. Mikhailov, Ye. Izrailev, and M. Schechner. It was built in 1966—70.

Railings of the Summer Gardens from the Neva 104

The Fontanka by night
105

107
Moscow Railway Station

107. In 1851, the architect Konstantin Thon, a representative of the mid-19th-century eclectic trend in architecture, built identical terminals at either end of what was once called the Nikolayevskaya Railway (now the October Railway), which linked St. Petersburg with Moscow. The terminals in both cities shared the name Nikolayevsky Station and both were decorated in the style of Renaissance architecture.

In 1959—60, the Leningrad terminal, now called the Moscow Station, was completely modernized and enlarged at the expense of a new building put up on Ligovsky Prospekt.

The façade of the main building overlooking Vosstaniya Square retains its original aspect.

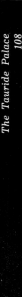

Theatre Square with the Kirov Opera
and Ballet Theatre (right)
109

110. The original design of the Catholic Church of St. Catherine belonged to P. Trezzini, who suggested to set it farther back from the road and to build two identical three-storey apartment houses on either side. The houses were eventually erected to his design, but the church itself was built by Vallin de la Mothe. In 1783, the construction works were supervised by Antonio Rinaldi.

111. The Bankovsky (Bank) Bridge over the Griboyedov Canal was built in 1825—26 by Georges Traitteur. The cast-iron abutments securing the cables by which the span of the bridge is anchored are embedded in the masonry of the embankment and hidden from view by cast-iron figures of fantastic gryphons modelled by Pavel Sokolov.

By day, too, Leningrad is an imposing sight from the air. The Neva may display a whole rainbow of colours — from the deep blue of our golden autumn to the dazzling white of winter. It is fascinating to have a bird's-eye view of this mighty river and builder (indeed, it formed the numerous

islands on which Leningrad is built). Later, when you walk along the Neva's quays and stand at the very edge of the water, you can feel the friendly handgrip of this extraordinary river, this half-river, half-strait that connects the huge Lake Ladoga with the Baltic.

*Railings of the Institute
of Finance and Economics.
Detail
112*

*Kamenny (Stone) Bridge across
the Griboyedov Canal
113*

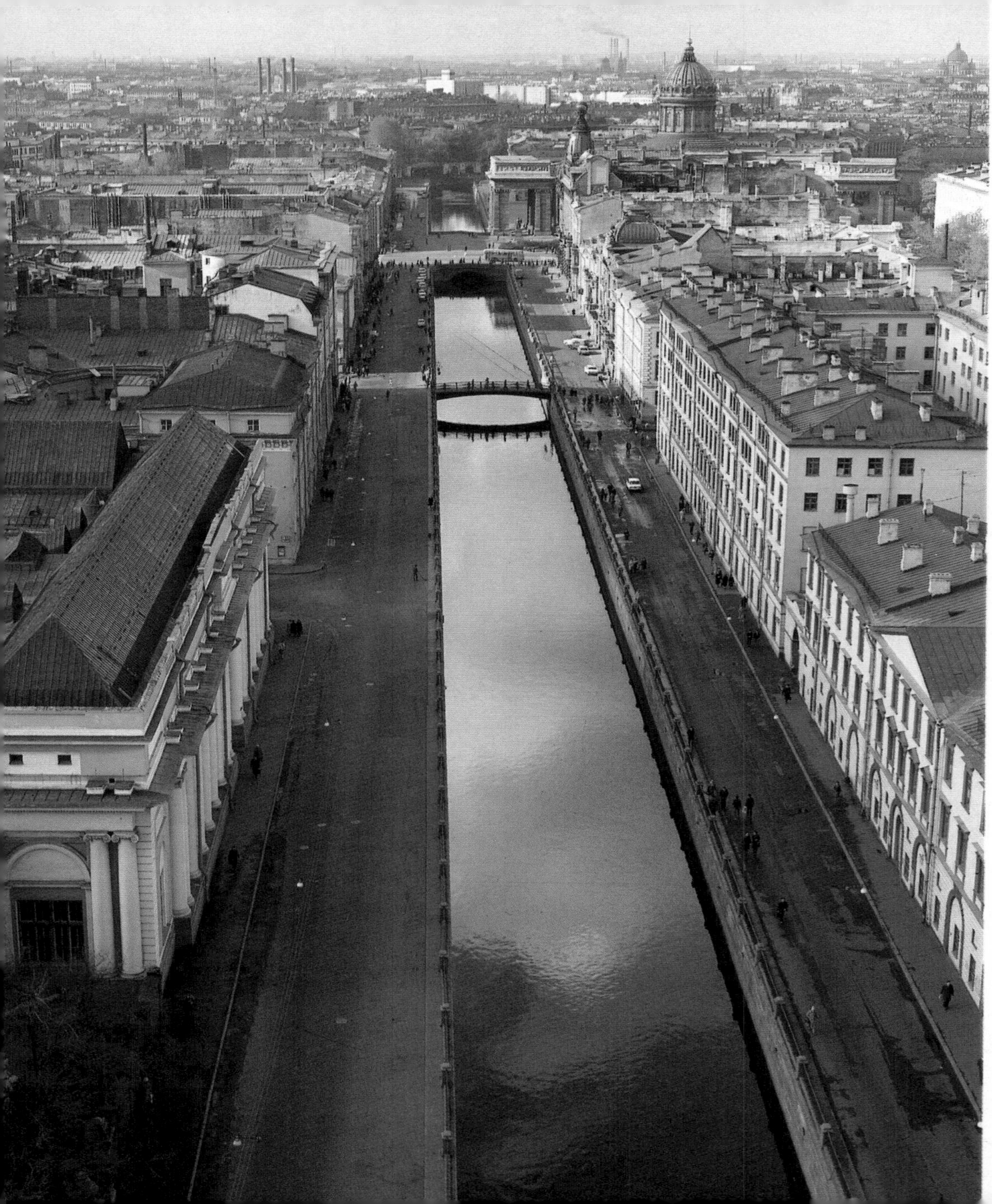

Griboyedov Canal

113, 114. The Griboyedov Canal, known in the past as the Yekaterininsky Canal, was laid out along the course of a small stream called the Krivusha. The digging of the canal began in 1764 and was completed in 1790, and the adjoining area was drained. Later, the canal's banks were sheathed in granite, and it became a useful city's waterway. In 1766, a stone bridge was built across the canal: Kazansky Bridge, which carries Nevsky Prospekt, and in 1766, Kamenny (Stone) Bridge carrying Dzerzhinsky Street.

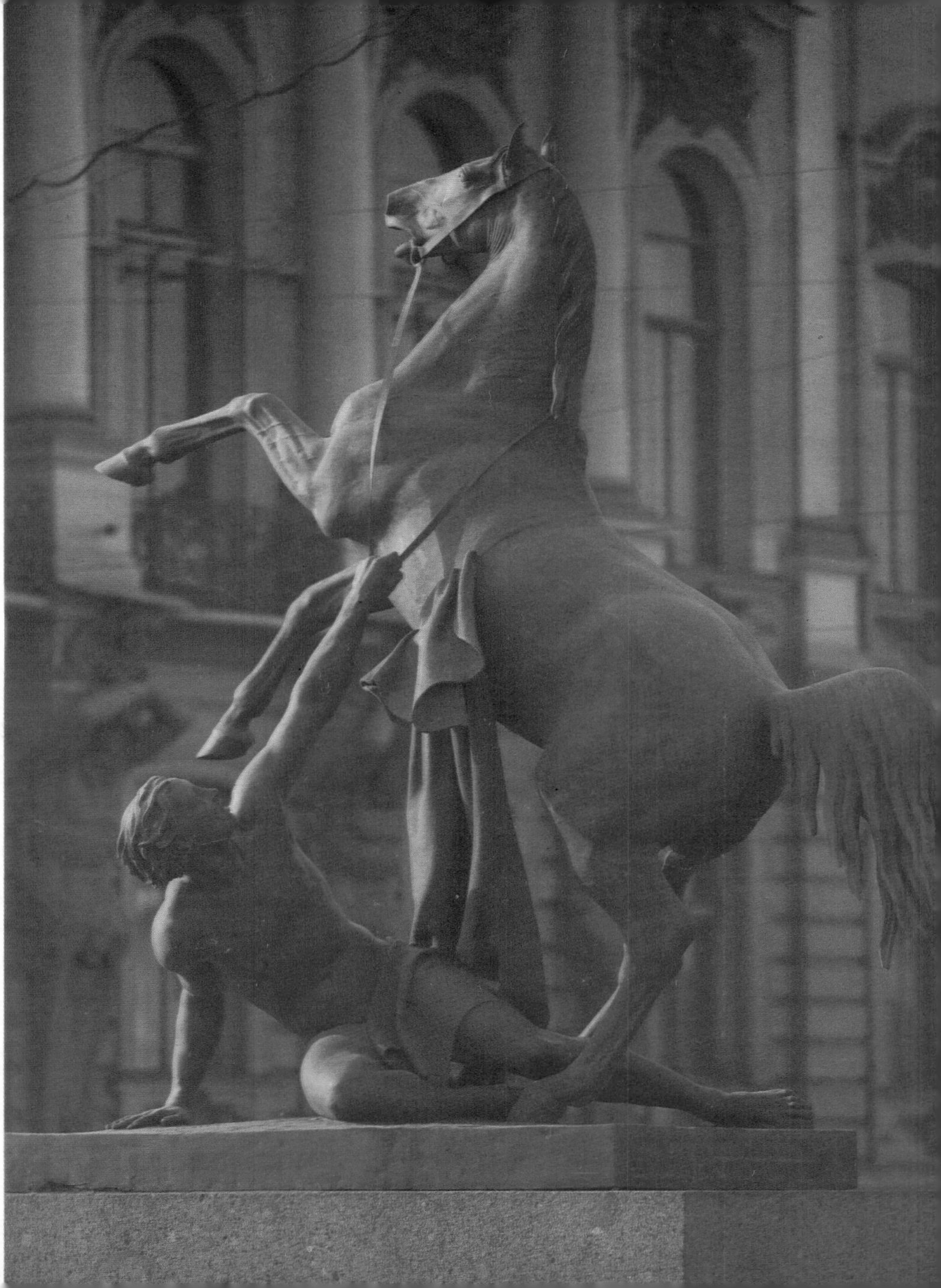

117

Equestrian group,
Horse Tamer, *on Anichkov Bridge*

While you are still in the air, note one interesting feature. Not one, but two completely different cities lie below you. One is dense and crowds in along the river's banks and on its islands. It comprises broad avenues and narrow streets that fan geometrically out to the east and south-east from the city's heart, the Admiralty. Here,

117. The Anichkov Bridge over the Fontanka is one of the most beautiful in Leningrad. It was built in 1839—41 by Andrei Gotman. The cast-iron railings are from a drawing by Karl Friedrich Schinkel. The bridge is adorned by four sculptural groups of horse tamers by Piotr Klodt.

118. The Palace of the Princess Beloselsky-Belozersky was designed in 1846 by Andrei Stakenschneider, who followed 18th-century examples of the Russian Baroque style in architecture, such as the Stroganov Palace and the Sheremetev Palace.
The building is decorated with colonnaded porticos, window surrounds of intricate pattern, and atlantes modelled by D. Jenssen.

garbed in the raiments of past centuries, the squat houses squeeze together, elbow to elbow; these are the city's venerable centenarians. It is a pleasure to walk along the streets in this section and admire the rich diversity of the façades with their porticos and caryatids. But their courtyards are narrow and dark, and their dimly-lit

Lamps decorating Italian Bridge

Now the building houses the District Committee of the CPSU.

120. The Church of the Resurrection of Christ also known as the Church of the Saviour on the Spilled Blood, a picturesque multi-domed pseudo-Russian building, was erected to the design of Alfred Parland between 1883 and 1907 on the spot, where Alexander II was assassinated. The church, with its ornate decoration — different kinds of stone, gilded details and mosaic panels — combined with variously shaped cupolas, is in no way attuned to its classic environment.
The mosaic panels decorating the façades and interior of the church were executed after sketches by Victor Vasnetsov, Mikhail Nesterov, Nikolai Bruni, Andrei Riabushkin, and others.

121. The building of the museum attached to the Stieglitz School of Technical Drawing (now the Mukhina School of Art and Industry) was erected in 1885—95 to the design of Maximilian Messmacher. It may well be called the most perfect example of an eclectic trend characteristic of Western European architecture in the second half of the 19th century. Messmacher mixed here elements of Baroque and Renaissance, and in addition designed the interiors to suit the character of museum exhibits on display: the Venetian Hall, Gothic Hall, Old Russian Hall, etc.

121
The Mukhina School
of Art and Industry

122
Vitebsk Railway Station

back stairways are straight out of Zola, Dickens, Nekrasov, or Dostoyevsky. Now they have to be rebuilt. There are many such districts in many of the large cities of the world; like any tourist, you will hardly notice them as you hurry from the Senate (built by Carlo Rossi) to the Admiralty (built by Adrian Zakharov)...

122, 123. The Vitebsk Station (the former Tsarskoselsky Station), built by Stanislaw Brzozowski and Semion Minash in 1902—4, represents a remarkable example of Russian Art Nouveau. This building, standing on Zagorodny Prospekt, replaced the old one, serving as the terminal of the first railway linking St. Petersburg with Tsarskoye Selo (now Pushkin).
The largest bookshop in Leningrad, the House of Books designed by Pavel Siuzor, and a food shop erected by Gavriil Baranovsky for the merchant Yeliseyev in 1902—3 are also typical Art Nouveau structures. The latter building contains a spacious auditorium (now the Leningrad Comedy Theatre).

If, on some bright morning, you come by ship into the mouth of the Neva, you will already have seen, many miles ahead of you over the low-lying haze of endless buildings, several tall "verticals", as the architects call them. The first to catch your eye will undoubtedly be the relatively low but impressive St. Isaac's Cathedral, whose gold dome rises a hundred metres into the sky, and which was once Russia's main cathedral. A hundred metres is not very tall, but the Neva has so flattened out the land here, at its mouth, that this golden helmet can be seen far away. During the War of 1941—45 (Great Patriotic War), the city's defenders, as they kept watch in their observation posts, could see St. Isaac's in their range-finders and take some cheer from it.

"Old St. Isaac's! It's still standing. Well, we can do it, too!"

During the war, the dome did not shine gold; a grey protective cover had been laid over it. But the main thing is that it stood!

If you take a look through some binoculars, you can see, a little to the left of St. Isaac's, a golden, dagger-like spire. This is the famous Sts Peter and Paul Cathedral. The spire is not only 150 years older than St. Isaac's; it is also twenty-two metres higher. For years, it was considered Europe's highest structure — the spires of Cologne Cathedral, which are higher, are of later date.

If you look more closely through your binoculars, you will see, side by side with the golden spire, a lacework tower. This is a television tower, a modern structure so light and airy that, even though it is two and a half times taller than the bell-tower of the Cathedral of Sts Peter and Paul, it becomes visible only when you get much closer to it.

I have mentioned these three highest points of Leningrad's skyline not for the sake of comparing their dimensions. These structures represent three sharply contrasting epochs in the life of Petersburg — Petrograd — Leningrad. The spire of the Sts Peter and Paul Cathedral dates to the city's infancy, and is thus a symbol of the period when not many people in Russia believed in the city's future, when more believed in its eventual abandonment.

The gold dome of St. Isaac's symbolizes a turning-point in the city's history. It represents the peak in the Romanovs' fortunes, yet it also marks the beginning of the end, the beginning of the long descent, which ended so abruptly in 1917.

Finally, the delicate and elegant television tower (316 metres high) is, though perhaps too "utilitarian" when compared to the others, not only the twentieth century and not only the Soviet Union. It is the post-war period, the period of the city's most rapid growth.

But all around the city's overcrowded centre stretches yet another city, a new city, which is constantly rising and moving out toward the countryside.

There are no porticos and no caryatids here. Here, as in many modern cities, glass and concrete reign supreme.

The houses no longer fall into endless ranks, as if in obedience to a silent command. The newly built apartment blocks are freely scattered about an area much larger than that of the Petersburg of 1703—1917. Not all the old-time residents like the glass and concrete or the plain geometric lines of the new buildings, similar all over the world, too often lacking character.

When you visit us, remember my advice: try, especially in the evening, to drive slowly through these new residential areas, where the buildings have just been completed and where the occupants are still settling in. Just think: not a single empty flat; all in all, millions of Leningraders!

A sphinx decorating Egyptian Bridge

A sphinx decorating Egyptian Bridge

The upper part of St. Isaac's Cathedral
126

127
TV tower

*Bell-tower of
the Cathedral of
Sts Peter and Paul* 125

*New residential district.
Pionerstroi Street*
130

*Volodarsky Bridge across
the Neva*
131

131. The two squares
situated near Volo-
darsky Bridge on either
bank of the Neva form
a beautiful archi-
tectural ensemble.
They were laid out
by Yevgeny Levinson,
Igor Fomin, and Da-
vid Goldgor, the left-
bank one in the early
1960s.

ГРАЖДАНЕ! ПРИ АРТОБСТРЕЛЕ ЭТА СТОРОНА УЛИЦЫ НАИБОЛЕЕ ОПАСНА

В ПАМЯТЬ О ГЕРОИЗМЕ И МУЖЕСТВЕ ЛЕНИНГРАДЦЕВ В ДНИ 900-ДНЕВНОЙ БЛОКАДЫ ГОРОДА СОХРАНЕНА ЭТА НАДПИСЬ.

The memorial inscription on the wall of a Leningrad house 135

135. This memorial inscription on the wall of a Leningrad house is preserved to remind passers-by of the War of 1941—45 when the city was subjected to severe shelling.

Leningrad is young, much younger than the majority of European cities; it is not yet three hundred years old. But it has been the scene of so many historical events of worldwide significance that it can stand comparison with the most celebrated and time-honoured capitals.

It is sufficient to mention two such events. It was here, in Leningrad, then Petrograd, that the October Revolution of 1917 which decided the future of Russia took place. It was Leningrad, the Hero City, that withstood the 900-day siege during the war of 1941—45.

Memorial to the Heroic Defenders of Leningrad. Sculptural groups: Sailors, Soldiers and Building of Defences

134, 136—138. The Memorial to the Heroic Defenders of Leningrad, commemorating those who saved their city from enemy occupation in the War of 1941—45, is the work of Mikhail Anikushin, Sergei Speransky, and Valentin Kamensky. The majestic architectural and sculptural ensemble was erected near the former front line. A broken ring of granite symbolizes the 900-day blockade of Leningrad. In the centre of the open area, forty metres in diameter, formed by the ring, is a bronze sculptural group entitled *Blockade*. In the image of the Mother is concentrated the anguish and the wrath of all women who mourn the loss of their children.

In the centre of the memorial is the 50-metre obelisk and the sculptural group, *The Victors*.

Placed on pylons flanking the wide flights of steps are the sculptural groups, *Soldiers, Sailors, Building the Defences, Casters*, and *People's Volunteers*, which embody the resolution and unconquerability of the Soviet people.

The memorial was inaugurated on May 9, 1975, on Victory Square.

139. The obelisk "To the Hero-City of Leningrad" on Vosstaniya Square was unveiled on May 9, 1985, to commemorate the 40th anniversary of the Victory in the War of 1941—45 (A. Alymov, V. Ivanov, architects; B. Rudno, engineer; B. Petrov, V. Sveshnikova, A. Charkina, sculptors).

140—142. The memorial in the Piskariovskoye Cemetery, designed by Alexander Vasilyev and Yevgeny Levinson, commemorates the courage and fortitude displayed by the people of Leningrad in the War of 1941—45. The bronze figure epitomizing the Motherland was modelled by Vera Isayeva and Robert Taurit. Two pavilions with solemn and laconic inscriptions by Mikhail Dudin on their walls house an exhibition devoted to the heroic 900-day defence of Leningrad. They serve as

Piskariovskoye Memorial Cemetery. The main avenue
140

Piskariovskoye Memorial Cemetery. The Flame of Remembrance
141

Piskariovskoye Memorial Cemetery.
Statue symbolizing the Motherland

propylaea that form the entrance into the necropolis. Buried in the cemetery are 420 thousand city's inhabitants and 50 thousand soldiers more than half of who perished during the 900-day siege of Leningrad. In the centre of a granite square enframed by a parapet is a bowl with the Flame of Remembrance. From here a flight of stairs leads to the mass graves and the statue of the Motherland. Behind the statue and on both sides of it are massive stelae of grey granite. Carved on the central stela are the words of a solemn epitaph by Olga Bergholz. The epitaph is flanked with high reliefs on themes from the life and defence of the besieged city. They were executed by M. Weinman, B. Kapliansky, A. Malakhin, and M. Kharlamova. The memorial was inaugurated on May 9, 1960.

I will say no more. Take a plane or board a ship and come to Leningrad, the city of scientific institutions, numerous museums, huge wharves and large factories.

143
Pribaltiiskaya Hotel

144
Palace of Youth

145

The Pulkovo Airport

Statue of Admiral Krusenstern
146

143. This seventeen-floor block of the hotel Pribaltiiskaya was built in 1979 by the architects N. Baranov, S. Yevdokimov, V. Kovaliova, and the engineer P. Panfilov. The first building erected on the Gulf of Finland shore of Vasilyevsky Island, it was intended to be the dominant structure of the future seafront district.

144. The Palace of Youth designed by P. Prokhorov, V. Tropin, A. Izoitko, and V. Pershin was built in the 1970s. It was intended for events like youth congresses, friendly talks and discussions, athletic competitions, performances, and young people's parties.

145. The Pulkovo Airport was designed by A. Zhuk, G. Vlanin, V. Maximov, and others and erected in 1973. It is a flat prismatic structure topped by five frustum-shaped glazed towers. The latter are visible a great way off and are an organic part of the port's silhouette.

146. The statue of Admiral Krusenstern, the first Russian circumnavigator of the globe, was cast from a model by Ivan Schroeder (the pedestal was designed by Hippolyte Monighetti) and put up in 1870—73 on the bank of the Neva opposite the Naval School (now the Frunze Naval Staff College). Krusenstern was a cadet of this school and, later, its Director.

Several magnificent suburbs encircle Leningrad — Pavlovsk, Pushkin, Petrodvorets, and Lomonosov, to name only a few. Each of these Russian Versailles and Fontainebleaus is well worth a visit.

It must, however, be admitted that for all the historic significance of each of these monuments of old, for all the numerous events, grand or tragic, that took place in the splendid palaces, amidst the greenery of the densely treed parks or on the banks of the ponds and tranquil rivulets sung by poets, the Leningrader of today visits most of them simply because he is in love with their beauty.

Of course, the town that bears Pushkin's name (and formerly known as Tsarskoye Selo) is dear to our hearts because of the wondrous genius of the Russian poet who lived here and once said that Tsarskoye Selo would for him forever remain a symbol of the motherland. It is, however, first and foremost their radiant and elegant beauty that lures us to the towns of Pushkin, Gatchina, Pavlovsk, Petrodvorets, and Lomonosov. There is beauty here to suit all tastes. Petrodvorets has its formal parks and its sedate early eighteenth-century architecture; Pavlovsk, its intricately winding rivulets and picturesque dales and hillocks. The architectural genius of Charles Cameron succeeded in creating here a masterpiece of romantic English landscape gardening.

Pushkin. The Lyceum (now, the All-Union Pushkin Memorial Museum)

150
Pushkin. The Turkish Bath Pavilion

151
Pushkin.
The Girl with a Pitcher fountain

152
Pushkin. The Creaky Summer-house

155   Pushkin. The Upper Bath Pavilion

147—155.
Town of Pushkin
The Great (Catherine) Palace, a remarkable monument of Russian 18th-century culture, is the compositional centre of the architectural and park ensemble of the town of Pushkin (formerly Tsarskoye Selo). Among those who took part in its creation were the Russian architects Alexei Kvasov and Savva Chevakinsky, as well as numerous artists, sculptors, and craftsmen.

The palace was completed by Bartolommeo Rastrelli in 1752—56. Its façade, which is over 300 metres long, has a rich and varied décor.

In the 1780s, some of Rastrelli's interiors were redecorated by Charles Cameron in the Classical style. After the fire of 1820 Vasily Stasov was called to remedy the damage caused to the Catherine Palace. He restored Rastrelli's and Cameron's interiors and created some new ones. Following the October Revolution the palaces and parks of Tsarskoye Selo were taken over by the state. The Catherine Palace became a museum of art and history, the parks were turned into areas of rest and recreation for the public. In 1937, the town was renamed Pushkin in honour of the great Russian poet, who spent his school years (1811—17) at the Lyceum in Tsarskoye Selo.

With the outbreak of war in 1941 the Soviet Government ordered the museum's collections evacuated inland. The town was captured by the enemy in September 1941. The Nazi soldiers ransacked the palace, and before retreating in January 1944 set it on fire.

German troops also caused heavy damage to the parks: the pavilions and bridges were destroyed, the trees wantonly cut down. Soviet restorers have brought the Catherine Palace and parks back to life.

The parks of Pushkin rank among the finest creations of Russian landscape gardening. They were laid out by Savva Chevakinsky, Bartolommeo Rastrelli, Vasily Neyelov, Yury Velten, Charles Cameron, and Adam Menelaws, the landscape gardeners Jan Roosen, Joseph Busch, and T. Ilyin at about the time the Catherine Palace was being built. Tens of thousands of serfs took part in their construction.

In 1780—94, Cameron erected an outstanding classical ensemble on Catherine Park's grounds including the Cold Baths, the Agate Rooms, the Promenade Gallery, the Hanging Garden, and a gently sloping ramp. In 1900, a monument to Pushkin by Roman Bach was unveiled in the Lyceum Garden. In the Catherine Park memories of Pushkin are evoked by the Lyceists' Walk and the sculpture *Girl with a Pitcher* by Pavel Sokolov, to which the poet dedicated one of the lyrics.

The Catherine Palace was fronted by the formal part of the park, which in the late 18th century began to undergo a gradual transformation, losing much of its original aspect. After the War of 1941—45 it was decided to restore the formal section from 18th-century drawings. The park stands out for straight avenues flanked with mighty century-old trees, green plots, and white marble statuary, the mirror-smooth waters of Big Lake with its green banks and shoreline architecture — the Hermitage and the Grotto (by Bartolommeo Rastrelli), the Admiralty and Marble Bridge (by Vasily Neyelov). In the 1770s, memorials were erected on its grounds dedicated to the victories in the Russo-Turkish war of 1768—74: the Orlov Gate and the Chesme Column by Antonio Rinaldi, the Kagul Obelisk by Yury Velten, and others. The Alexander Park is one of the largest landscape parks in the country, though the part that borders on the Catherine Park has to a certain degree retained its regular lay-out.

156—164. Pavlovsk

The Pavlovsk Palace is an architectural monument of the late 18th and first quarter of the 19th century brought into being by the joint efforts of outstanding architects and sculptors.

The palace's design, typical of the suburban mansions of the period, was by Charles Cameron, who put up the central block in 1782—86. In 1796—99, Vincenzo Brenna enlarged the complex by adding two symmetrically disposed service blocks and a palace church. He also created some new interiors: the Picture Gallery, the Throne Room, and others. In 1803, the central block was damaged by fire.

The restoration of the interiors was entrusted to Andrei Voronikhin who elaborated and partially altered their décor. Together with Giacomo Quarenghi, Voronikhin was responsible for the lay-out and decoration of the ground floor.

The last in the line of talented architects who worked in Pavlovsk was Carlo Rossi. He designed the Corner Drawing-room in 1816 and the Palace Library in 1822—24.

The combined efforts of all these architects plus those of the sculptors (Ivan Prokofyev, Ivan Martos, Mikhail Kozlovsky, Vasily Demuth-Malinovsky) and the artists (Giovanni Battista Scotti, Johann Mettenleiter, Andrei Martynov, and Pietro Gonzaga) brought into being a complete, integrated architectural complex. Notwithstanding the participation of so many artists in the construction and decoration of the palace, it demonstrates an amazing stylistic unity illustrating the evolution of Classicism in Russian architecture in the late 18th and first quarter of the 19th century.

After the October Revolution, a museum of history and art was organized on the palace premises.

During the War of 1941—45 Pavlovsk was occupied by Nazi troops. Before retreating they burnt the palace down and caused heavy damage to the park. Today, both the palace and the park have been completely restored.

The museum has on display unique works of art. The collection of antique sculpture housed in the palace ranks among the richest in the country, second only to that of the Hermitage.

Picture gallery boasts many canvases by well-known Western European artists of the 17th and 18th centuries. There is also a superb collection of tapestries and *objets d'art* in bronze, ivory, and valuable minerals.

The Pavlovsk Park (600 hectares) was created by the famous Russian architects of the late 18th and early 19th century, in the course of fifty years, beginning from 1777. It is one of the most beautiful landscape parks in the world. Many of the park's pavilions put up in the 1780s and '90s were designed by Cameron, among them the Temple of Friendship, the Apollo Colonnade, the Aviary, the Pavilion of the Three Graces, and others. Erected in the early 19th century were Visconti and Peel-Tower Bridges designed by Voronikhin, Cast-iron Bridge and the Rossi Pavilion by Rossi, and Paul's Mausoleum by Thomas de Thomon.

In spite of its having been created over a period of fifty years by a succession of architects, the park is compositionally an integral ensemble.

159
Pavlovsk.
The Great Palace with Centaur
Bridge in the foreground

Pavlovsk. The Aviary
160

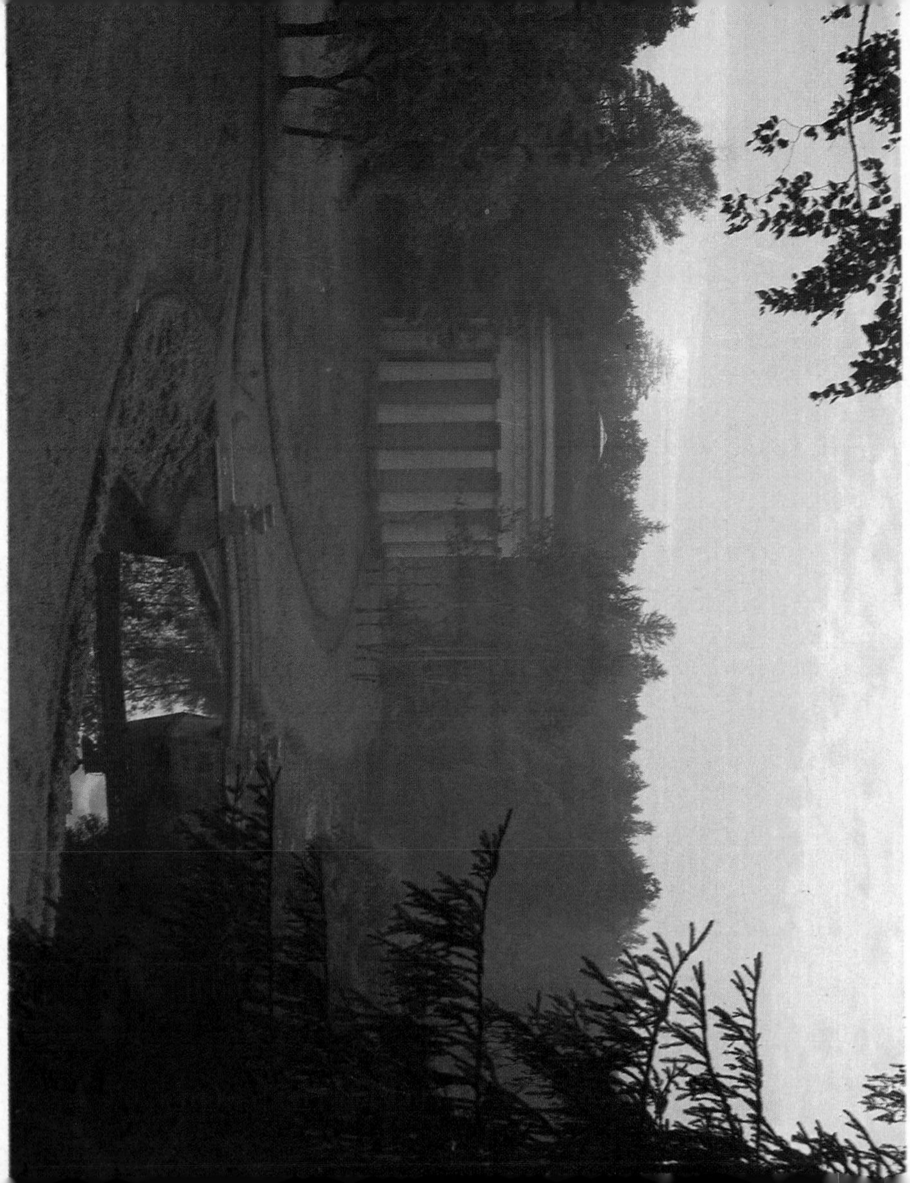

Pavlovsk. The Temple of Friendship
161

163
Pavlovsk.
The Slavianka River valley

PETRODVORETS

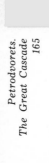

Petrodvorets.
The Great Cascade
165

Petrodvorets.
The Sirens fountain
166

168
Petrodvorets. The Marly Palace

169
*Petrodvorets.
The Hermitage
Pavilion*

170
*Petrodvorets.
The Sea Canal
seen from
the Great Palace*

171
*Petrodvorets.
The Samson
fountain*

Petrodvorets. The Monplaisir Palace
172

173 Petrodvorets. Dragons decorating
the Chessboard Hill Cascade

174
Petrodvorets. The Sheaf fountain

Petrodvorets.
The Chessboard
Hill Cascade
175

165—175. Petrodvorets

Petrodvorets, formerly called Peterhof, is one of the magnificent park-and-palace complexes in the vicinity of Leningrad. Situated on the coast of the Gulf of Finland, it was intended to symbolize the power and the glory of Russia and its consolidation on the liberated Slavic shores of the Baltic after the Great Northern War.

Its splendid palaces and exquisite pavilions, its beautiful gardens and parks, its picturesque fountains and cascades are the creations of talented architects, landscape gardeners, sculptors, and artists. The complex, which was started in the early 18th century and completed in the mid-19th century, shows the aesthetic features of Russian architecture characteristic of that time. In Soviet time, all the royal palaces were converted into museums and all the parks into rest and recreation areas for the working people. The first group of visitors, over 500 persons in all, entered the halls of the Great Palace as early as May 1918.

During the War of 1941—45 the Nazi invaders reduced the Great Palace to a heap of rubble and inflicted enormous damage to most of the other structures of Petrodvorets. Restoration work on the palace was begun as soon as the town was liberated.

At present the Petrodvorets complex comprises three parks — the Upper Park, Lower Park and Alexandria Park, with their six museums, 147 fountains, three cascades, and other structures.

The Great Palace is finely situated on a high natural mound. Several architects took part in its construction: Johann-Friedrich Braunstein, Jean-Baptiste Le Blond and Niccolo Michetti in 1714—23; Bartolommeo Francesco Rastrelli in 1747—55; and Andrei Stakenschneider in 1847. Its southern facade overlooks the Upper Park whose formal lay-out is organically linked with the compositional scheme of the palace. The northern slope of the mound, on which the palace stands, is adorned with terraces, two monumental stairways, and the Great Cascade, which is linked with the Sea Canal flowing into the gulf. The Great Cascade was designed by Le Blond, Braunstein, Michetti, and Mikhail Zemtsov in 1715—24. The centrepiece of the Great Cascade, *Samson Rending Open the Jaws of a Lion,* stolen by the Nazis during their occupation of the town, was recreated by the Soviet sculptor Vasily Simonov in 1947.

Flanking the Great Cascade at its foot are the two Voronikhin Colonnades, built by that architect in 1800—4.

In accordance with the formal garden rules, all fountains, cascades and park pavilions are arranged symmetrically on either side of the Sea Canal: the Chessboard Hill Cascade in the eastern part of the Park corresponds to the Golden Hill Cascade in the western part, the Monplaisir Palace — to the Hermitage Pavilion, the Adam fountain — to the Eve fountain. The Sea Canal itself is embellished with 22 fountains.

The Monplaisir Palace, erected on the shore of the Gulf of Finland in 1714—23 by Braunstein, Le Blond, and Michetti, is one of the earliest structures built in the Lower Park.

The Hermitage Pavilion was constructed in 1721—26 by Braunstein. The moat surrounding it emphasizes its solitary aspect.

The Marly Palace at the west end of the Lower Park was built to the plans of Braunstein in 1721—23.

The landscape Alexandria Park was laid out in 1826 by Adam Menelaws. The Cottage Pavilion, designed by the same architect, displays the elements of the pseudo-Gothic style.

The Petrodvorets water-supply system, built in the early 18th century by the hydraulic engineer Vasily Tuvolkov, the architects Mikhail Zemtsov and I. Ustinov, is unique: unlike the fountains of European parks which were fed by machinery, utilized here is the natural decline of the terrain from the Ropsha Heights (22 kilometres from Petrodvorets) to the sea. Ground waters gather into fourteen reservoirs by way of canals, then flow to the fountains through pipes. The pressure of the water is so strong that the jet of *Samson*, the park's main fountain, shoots up to a height of 22 metres.

176—179.

Town of Lomonosov

The architectural ensemble of the town of Lomonosov (formerly Oranienbaum) consists of the Great Palace, the Chinese Palace, the Palace of Peter III and the Coasting Hill Pavilion. Up to 1917 the palaces of Oranienbaum served as the summer residences of the royal family and aristocracy. After the October Revolution they were declared the property of the people. The parks were turned into recreation areas, the palaces into museums.

The Great Palace was built between 1711 and 1727 by Mario Giovanni Fontana and Gottfried Schädel.

The Chinese Palace was designed by Antonio Rinaldi and built in 1762—68. Rinaldi's project was implemented by talented folk craftsmen — moulders, marblers, mosaicists, wood-carvers. The Hall of the Muses and the Grand Hall, the Lilac Drawing-room, the Buglework and Gold Rooms are especially striking for the rich variety of their décor. The palace's ceilings were painted by well-known Italian masters of the Venetian academic school.

The name, Chinese Palace, stems from the *chinoiserie* décor in four of its rooms. The palace's unique parquetry, which was executed after Rinaldi's drawings by Russian craftsmen, has survived to our day.

The Palace of Peter III was built in 1758—62 by Rinaldi. The rooms of the top floor are richly decorated. Especially interesting is the Picture Gallery reconstructed after the 1941—45 War.

The unique collection of porcelain, furniture and woodcarvings is also an integral part of the décor.

The Coasting Hill Pavilion was erected in 1762—74 by Rinaldi. Originally there was a sloping roadway running down from the pavilion along which special cars took people for amusement rides. In the 19th century, the roadway fell into decay and was dismantled. The light, slender silhouette of the building blends harmoniously with the surrounding landscape. Radiant and beautiful are the pavilion's interiors — the Circular Hall, the Porcelain and White Rooms, with their ornamental painting and stuccowork.

Lomonosov.
The Coasting
Hill Pavilion
176

Lomonosov. Petrovsky Bridge
179

Now, however, yet another ring encircles the city. It is with good reason called the Green Belt of Glory, and it runs along the areas where, between 1941 and 1944, Hitler's armies stood poised to seize Leningrad, where, in January 1944, the near-encirclement was broken through.

Lake Razliv
180

181—183. The Green Belt of Glory is a memorial complex dedicated to the heroic defence of Leningrad during the War of 1941—45. The total length of the memorial "belt" is 220 kilometres. It includes the Road of Life, the Oranienbaum bridgehead, and towns and villages located in the area of the former front line. 45 similar milestones mark every kilometre on the Road of Life between Leningrad and Lake Ladoga. This was the name given to the route, one hundred kilometres long, which during the siege of Leningrad linked the city with the Osinovets Cape on Lake Ladoga, and when the lake was frozen, with the small village of Kobon on the eastern shore of the lake. Placed on pedestals and installed along the "belt" are tanks, guns, and trucks raised from the bottom of Lake Ladoga, which supplied the besieged city with food and munitions and helped to evacuate the starving Leningraders — children, women and old people — to the "mainland".

The Flower of Life memorial, designed by A. Levenkov and P. Melnikov, was set up near the village of Kovaliovo in 1968.

The Katiusha memorial, designed by A. Levenkov, P. Melnikov and L. Chulkevich, was put up in 1966 near the village of Kornevo, on the spot where a battery defending the Road of

Life used to stand. Ka-
tiusha was a popular
wartime name of a lor-
ry-mounted multiple
rocket launcher.

The Broken Ring
Monument near Lake
Ladoga was executed
by K. Simun, V. Fi-
lippov, P. Melnikov,
and I. Rybin in 1966.
It was put up by re-
sidents of the Kalinin
district of Leningrad
between kilometres
39 and 40 of the Road
of Life, at the Vaga-
novo decline to Lake
Ladoga, where the
legendary route across
the ice began.

The gap in the arch
symbolizes the only
outlet from the be-
sieged city.

181
*The Road of Life.
The Flower of Life*

*The Road of Life.
The Broken Ring
Memorial*
183

The Road of Life. Katiusha
182

More than thirty memorials have been raised along this line, amidst quiet fields and forests, where over forty years ago the roar of explosions was deafening and people were dying. For 900 days and nights the people of Leningrad stood their ground, refusing to let the most horrendous blockade of all times strangle their city.

Even many books cannot do justice to the road that Leningrad has passed; nor can a whole gallery of paintings capture the many faces of the city. But each new word and every new photograph, if offered with love and truth, will add something to what we should know about the city. This book will have succeeded if it enables the people of Leningrad to look at their city anew and if it allows the first-time visitor to get acquainted with this wondrous city. This city — the city of Lenin, the city of the revolution, the heroic city of the war — deserves all the love that people have for it.

Lev Uspensky

186 *Nevsky Prospekt on a festive night*

187 *Nevsky Prospekt on a festive night*

188 *Festive fireworks*

Photographs by

Sergei Alexeyev and Valentin Baranovsky — *10, 15, 31, 36, 41, 61, 73, 75, 83, 97, 101, 106, 107, 111, 113, 119, 125, 126, 129, 132, 187*

Valery Barnev — *117, 179*

Yury Belinsky — *6, 18*

Leonid Bogdanov — *46*

Moisei Bytka — *48, 84, 112, 133*

Victor Vasilyev — *33, 95*

Vladimir Davydov — *151, 159*

Pavel Demidov and Oleg Trubsky — *47, 49, 131, 143*

Natalia and Konstantin Doka — *169, 170, 178*

Vladimir Dorokhov — *156*

Nikita Yegorov — *77*

Kira Zharinova and Vladimir Sobolev — *2, 3, 7, 16, 17, 35, 37, 38, 43, 53, 54, 55, 57, 58, 59, 60, 63, 64, 65, 66, 68, 69, 72, 78, 80, 81, 85, 86, 87, 88, 91, 93, 94, 96, 100, 121, 127, 136, 137, 138, 146, 149, 150, 152, 153, 155, 158, 161, 162, 167, 171, 173, 175, 184, 185, 186, 188*

Yevgeny Kassin — *40*

Romuald Kirillov — *19, 44, 144*

Romuald Kirillov and Leonard Kheifets — *98, 103*

Boris Kuzmin — *164*

Ferdinand Kuziumov — *74*

Boris Manushin — *21*

Vladimir Melnikov — *5, 8, 22, 25, 27, 28, 29, 32, 34, 45, 50, 52, 70, 71, 76, 79, 82, 90, 92, 102, 114, 116, 117, 118, 122, 123, 124, 128, 134, 142, 145, 154, 157, 160, 163, 172, 174, 181, 182*

Yevgeny Montlevich — *30, 42, 139, 140, 141, 148*

Valentin Nesterov — *39*

Victor Savik — *51, 180*

Vladimir Samoilov — *11, 130*

Vladimir Samoilov and Romuald Kirillov — *1, 9, 13*

Boris Smelov — *12, 176*

Boris Stezhka — *56, 62, 67*

Leonid Tarazevich — *165, 166, 168*

David Trakhtenberg — *135*

Sergei Falin — *4, 14, 20, 23, 26, 89, 99, 104, 105, 108, 109*

Grigory Khatin — *147*

Boris Cheremisin — *120*

Igor Yasevich — *110*

ЛЕНИНГРАД

Альбом (на английском языке)

Издательство «Аврора». Ленинград. 1987
Изд. № 1323. (7-80)
ЛПО «Типография имени Ивана Федорова»
Ленинград
Printed and bound in the USSR